Carol Armstrong's
Patches & Posies

DESIGNS FOR APPLIQUÉ & QUILTING

C&T PUBLISHING

Text and watercolors © 2006 Carol Armstrong

Artwork © 2006 C&T Publishing, Inc.

Publisher: Amy Marson

Editorial Director: Gailen Runge

Acquisitions Editor: Jan Grigsby

Editor: Lynn Koolish

Technical Editors: Teresa Stroin, Wendy Mathson

Copyeditor/Proofreader: Wordfirm, Inc.

Design Director/Cover and Book Designer: Christina D. Jarumay

Illustrator: Kirstie L. Pettersen

Production Assistant: Kiera Lofgreen

Photography: Luke Mulks

Published by C&T Publishing, Inc., P.O. Box 1456, Lafayette, CA 94549

Library of Congress Cataloging-in-Publication Data

Armstrong, Carol
    Carol Armstrong's Patches & posies : designs for appliqué & quilting /
Carol Armstrong.
        p. cm.
    Includes index.
    ISBN-13: 978-1-57120-353-3 (paper trade)
    ISBN-10: 1-57120-353-2 (paper trade)
    1. Appliqué--Patterns. 2. Quilting. 3. Fabric flowers. I. Title:
Patches and posies. II. Title.

TT779.A75976 2006
746.44'5041--dc22

2005033574

Printed in China

10 9 8 7 6 5 4 3 2 1

CONTENTS

INTRODUCTION

"I wandered lonely
as a cloud

That floats on high
o'er vales and hills,

When all at once
I saw a crowd,

A host, of golden
daffodils..."

William Wordsworth found the color of flowers an inspiration to pen this much-loved poem. I also find the color of flowers an inspiration. But I pick up a needle and thread and make quilts. In this book you will find patterns for 24 wonderful flowers to inspire you, including the golden daffodil.

Appliqué is the perfect technique to create quilts filled with flowers. Let me show you a relaxed, template-free method of hand appliqué using a lightbox. Use my simple appliquéd patch style to accent your flowers with more color and add some of those traditional patchwork designs we all love.

For fun, why not try some embellishment options? A bead, a button, a touch of lace, some fancy yarn, a dab of paint, and some fabric fringe are among the many ideas I have included to get you started. Then let your imagination run!

And, of course, there is the quilting. Let me free you from static designs so you can enjoy the beauty of shadows and lines created by random patterns—and with little or no marking. The possibilities are endless.

So follow your stitching muse. Wordsworth ends,

"And then my heart with pleasure fills, and dances with the daffodils."

Enjoy!

Tools and Materials

TOOLS

Lightbox

My method of appliqué uses a lightbox to make the tracing of designs easier. Many sizes and styles are available in art, craft, and some quilt shops. As a substitute, you can use a window on a sunny day or a glass table with a low-wattage lamp underneath.

Needles

For appliqué, I use a size 10 milliner's needle, which is relatively long. Its length is good when needle-turning appliquéd edges. A straw needle is also a good option.

For embroidery, choose a needle with a large eye for easy threading of floss. I use sizes 8–10.

For quilting, I use a sharps size 10 for stitching without a frame or hoop. A betweens needle is best for the rocking motion if you quilt with a frame or hoop.

For basting, a long, large needle is nice for quick work.

Cutting Tools

For cutting out shapes, a large pair of good scissors works well. Keep them sharp.

For cutting threads and snipping into curves when appliquéing, a small pair of scissors that snips down to its tips is excellent.

For cutting borders and bindings, and squaring appliquéd panels, I suggest a rotary cutter, ruler, and gridded cutting mat.

Marking Tools

Many removable fabric marking pens and pencils are available. I use a standard wash-out or water-erasable blue fabric marker for most fabrics, and a white version for dark fabrics. Check your favorite quilt store for the options. I use these markers for both appliqué and quilting. They should come out easily with a little water. Always test a new pen or pencil for removability. Be sure to remove all marks before ironing, as the heat from the iron may make the marks impossible to remove.

 Tip A cotton swab dipped in water makes a good eraser for water-erasable marker and avoids wetting the whole piece.

Pins

Use short glass-headed pins to hold appliqué pieces in place as you stitch; because they are short, they stay out of your way as you appliqué. Standard silk pins are fine for all basic sewing tasks.

Thimble

I use a leather thimble on my pushing finger when quilting. Many different kinds of thimbles are available to protect your fingers. They all feel awkward at first, but a thimble is worth using. You may need to try several until you find the one that best suits your sewing style.

Iron

A good steam iron and a padded pressing surface are basic sewing tools. I press appliqué from the back on a folded white towel with some steam.

MATERIALS

Thread

Good thread makes nice stitches.

For appliqué, use cotton or cotton-wrapped polyester thread. Try to match the thread to the appliqué fabric as closely as possible in natural light. For a better match, lay a single strand of the thread across the fabric for comparison, rather than using the whole spool.

For basting, use a white cotton thread.

For quilting, use thread specifically designed for hand quilting. I have used many brands and have been happy with most of them. I use quilting thread with extra beeswax for sewing on beads.

For the flower details, use embroidery floss. I keep a wide palette of colors on hand.

Fabric

Where to begin? A trip to your local quilt shop is a good start. Lightweight 100% cotton fabrics are best for appliqué. Cotton fabric is very cooperative with simple finger-pressing and needle-turn appliqué. Good-quality fabrics create good-quality quilts.

I use an unbleached, preshrunk muslin for my backgrounds and backings. I like the way it shows off the quilted designs.

I do not prewash my fabrics, but I color test a small piece in a little warm water first if I suspect that the dye might run. If you will be washing the finished quilt you should prewash the fabrics.

Color? Your choices are many. For appliqué, I use solids, tone-on-tones, batiks, and other variegated or mottled shades. But don't skip looking at those larger prints. Cut a stencil of a leaf or petal and lay it in various places on a print. You may find just the right color in an unexpected place. You can also find color transitions that are perfect. For example, I cut crocus petals from printed lemons (see page 21).

For the border, binding, and appliquéd patches, select from any and all designs to coordinate with your flower colors.

I keep a nice stash of fabrics on hand for those last-minute choices. My stash is always growing and changing.

Batting

I use a needle-punched polyester batting. It is rather like a thin, light blanket. It is easy to hand quilt and it really highlights the quilted designs. You can also use a lightweight cotton batting suitable for hand quilting; it will be less dimensional than the polyester. Try a test square of each for comparison.

Embellishments

Who can resist the temptation of all the buttons, yarns, lace, and beads that are so readily available these days? Any flower with a circle center is a great candidate for a button. A bit of lace or decorative yarn can highlight your favorite flowers. Beads, craft wire, and faux suede add other creative possibilities. Don't forget about fussy cutting, either. Fussy cutting allows for color changes within a single appliquéd piece. Look at large prints for flower petals and leaves hiding within the pattern.

Play with your own combinations of embellishments and extras, prowl around knit shops for some fun ideas, and make each flower your very own!

Below is a list of materials, other than fabric, that I used for various embellishments. See projects and flower instructions for specific uses.

    Beads: seed beads, 6mm beads, bugle beads

    Ribbon: ⅛" wide, satin

    #5 perle cotton thread

    Craft wire: 28-gauge, gold colored

    Laces, tatting

    Yarns: chenille and specialty varieties

    Waxed thread

    Buttons

    Fabric paints

    Gel pens

    Faux suede

I also used the following:

    Fusible web to make some fringed fabric

    Washable glue stick to hold small items in place prior to sewing

    Wire snips

    Beeswax to strengthen thread for sewing on buttons and beads

Your list can include these items and more. Embellishment is all about trying new things.

Lightbox Appliqué Basics

This is appliqué made simple. I have eliminated the need for templates, freezer paper, or overlays. With a little preparation of the appliqué pieces, you get right to sewing.

PREPARING THE APPLIQUÉ

Draw or trace your appliqué pattern on plain white paper in black marker. If you are new to appliqué, work on a small project and enlarge a motif to avoid using very small pieces.

Secure your pattern to the lightbox with masking tape.

Cut the background fabric at least 1″ larger than the pattern on all sides. This extra allows for any shrinkage from the appliqué and can be trimmed after the appliqué is finished. Place the background fabric right side up on the lightbox, centering it on the pattern. Secure the fabric with tape or pins.

Use a removable fabric marker to trace the entire design onto the background fabric. Trace lightly, making sure the lines are dark enough to be easily seen. These lines are your guides when sewing the appliqué pieces. The numbers on the patterns indicate the order of the appliqué. Remove the marked background fabric but leave the pattern on the lightbox.

Choose the fabric for each piece to be appliquéd. Place the fabric right side up over the pattern. Use a removable marker to trace the exact line of the appliqué piece. Trace **all** around each piece. This line is your guide for turning under the allowance and is a reference for later pieces to be appliquéd.

 If you can't see the black line through your fabric, remove the fabric and the pattern from the lightbox and trace over the pattern on the paper with a red marker. (I use a Sharpie brand.) Take the pattern off the lightbox to do this, as the ink may bleed through the paper.

Cut out each piece ³⁄₁₆″ to ¼″ outside the marked line. A little extra is fine here. You can trim it if it is in your way when you stitch.

ORDER OF APPLIQUÉ

To help keep track of your pieces, mark the piece number in the seam allowance. This is helpful especially when pieces are the same color and are similar in shape.

Those pieces that are farthest away in the motif (in the background of the appliqué design) are sewn down first. Then you work forward. I have numbered the patterns with the order of appliqué to get you started; the order will become more apparent as you gain experience. Those pieces with no overlapping edges can be stitched down at any time in the sequence. Always allow plenty of turn-under allowance. It can be trimmed away if it's unneeded but it's useful if anything shifts during appliqué.

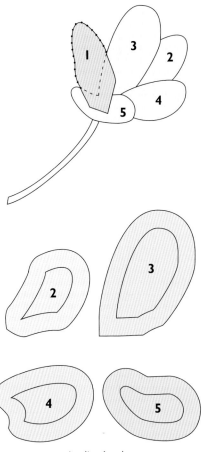

Appliqué order

Stitching

Begin stitching with the first piece. As you stitch, use the side of the needle to turn under the seam allowance to the line on the appliqué piece, matching the motif to the marked lines on the background. Use pins as needed to secure the piece and to keep it from shifting as you sew. Check often to make sure that the piece is lined up with the placement lines on the background.

Turn under only enough allowance to take a few stitches. Don't look too far ahead other than to check for placement. Allow your stitching to be close rather than perfect—the removable markings will disappear, and Mother Nature is always changing. Relax and look at the whole picture. Close is good.

Remember, only turn under and sew those edges that are not covered by another piece.

After the appliqué is finished, add the embroidered details.

 When stitching a flower, check for embellishment options first, as the order of appliqué may be interrupted by additions. It always helps to read through all the instructions before you begin.

PRESSING

Remove any marks and press the appliquéd piece from the back on a padded surface. Trim the background to the needed size after pressing. You can iron the piece from the back even with embellishments. Use several layers of terry towel between the appliqué and the ironing board so as not to crush any items. Do not overheat paint or any other heat-sensitive items.

 Never iron a marked piece; remove the marks first. The heat from the iron may set the marks and make them difficult or impossible to remove.

PRE-APPLIQUÉ

Pre-appliqué is effective when appliqué pieces meet along a continuous line of design. With this technique, two or more pieces of a motif are sewn to each other before they are applied to the background. Turning under the meeting edges is smoother and easier.

Pre-appliqué in the same manner and in the same order as any other appliqué. Do not stitch into the perimeter turn-under allowance so it will turn under easily when you sew the pieces to the background. Remember to change thread color as the fabric changes.

When the pieces are pre-appliquéd, stitch the group to the background as one piece. Clip any inside curves to ease turn-under. As you gain appliqué experience you will note when this method is beneficial. I have noted in the instructions where to pre-appliqué.

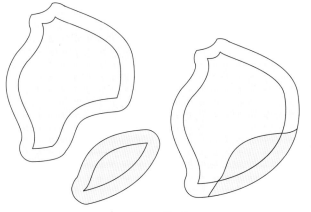

Pre-appliqué

APPLIQUÉ PATCHES

I enjoy the look of traditional pieced designs but prefer to appliqué them. Mark the design on the background with removable marker. Cut pieces with ³⁄₁₆″ added all around for every patch in the design. Pin a patch in place with the allowance evenly distributed. Turn under the allowance a little inside the marked line as you stitch it. This leaves a space between all the pieces, revealing the background. Your stitching does not have to be perfect, just close.

For patch motifs that will be parallel to two sides of the design, you may want to wait until you have sewn on the borders before adding the patches. I used this technique in the *Amaryllis in Red* project (see page 52). I found it was easier to keep things square this way. Just keep the work smooth and flat as you stitch the patches.

To use this method, finish the flower appliqué, remove all markings, and press. Trim the background to the size needed and add the borders. Return the piece to the pattern on the lightbox and mark the appliquéd patch design. Appliqué the patches, remove all markings, and press again.

 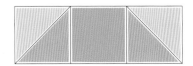 

Appliqué patches

THE APPLIQUÉ STITCH

Thread a size 10 milliner's needle with a single strand of thread, 12″–18″ long. A longer piece of thread will fray before you use it all. Knot the thread. Use the shaft of the needle to turn under the allowance of the appliqué piece to the marked line. Slip the knot into the fold of the turn-under by running the needle through the fold from the back of the piece and out onto the edge to be stitched down. This hides the knot in the fold. (See illustration on page 10.)

To avoid pushing the background fabric as you needle-turn the appliqué piece, keep the background fabric somewhat taut as you work. I sew with the piece on my leg (you can use a pillow on your lap if you prefer). The friction of the background fabric on my jeans is sufficient to hold it well. If you are stitching near the edge of the background it is helpful to pin the background fabric to your jeans (or pillow) to offer some resistance. You will have to turn and re-pin as you stitch the piece.

Place the piece to be appliquéd in position on the background. Use a few pins if necessary to hold it in place. Whenever possible, begin stitching at a spot on the appliqué shape that will give you a continuous line.

Insert the needle into the background, at a spot that is even with the thread's exit from the appliqué piece. With the needle still under the background, move the needle tip forward. Come up through the background and through a few threads on the folded edge of the appliqué piece. Pull the thread snug without drawing up the fabric.

Insert the needle into the background again, even with the thread's exit from the appliqué piece, and continue with another stitch. Turn your work as you sew to keep your stitches even and your wrist straight. Stitch away from yourself, or from right to left for right-handed sewers and from left to right for left-handers (like me).

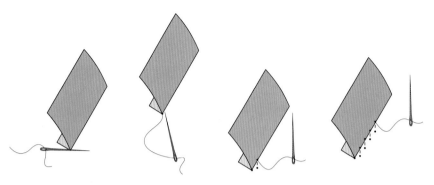

The appliqué stitch

The stitches will become small, even, and easy after a bit of practice.

To end, take three stitches in the same place, either from the front, where the stitches will be covered by the next appliqué piece, or from the back behind an appliquéd piece, through just the background fabric. Clip the thread.

Don't worry about little imperfections. Many will disappear when the appliqué is pressed. Relax and enjoy the process.

INSIDE CURVES

I try to avoid sharp inside curves whenever possible when designing a motif, but sometimes nature throws a curve you can't avoid, such as the hosta and marigold leaves (see pages 27 and 30).

Stitch around the piece until you are near the inner curve, then clip into the turn-under allowance a few threads shy of the marked line. Keep stitching down into the curve. When the fabric becomes difficult to turn, use your needle to turn under the allowance on the far side of the clip. Hold this in place. Continue by placing your needle under the appliqué. Pivot upward into the turn-under, rolling the allowance under, and stitch in place. Adjust the turn-under as close to the reference lines as you can. Remember that the lines will be erased. Allow yourself to let the piece change a bit from the original shape. As with many techniques, practice is helpful.

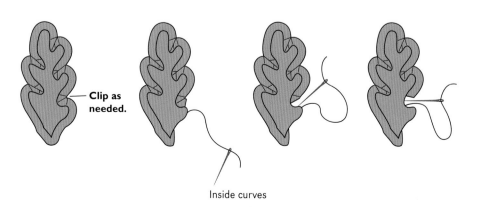

Clip as needed.

Inside curves

For gentle curves, clip often enough to allow the fabric to roll under easily. I do not clip outside curves. However, if you find one that is particularly uncooperative, a few clips may help. For small outside curves such as circles for flower centers, just stitch and turn slowly, taking one stitch at a time and then readjusting using the marked line on the background as your more important guide.

POINTS

Start at a point if that point meets a stem or a flower center, or if there is a point at both ends of an appliqué piece. Otherwise start on a smooth section of the piece.

Square off the end of the point, leaving an approximate ³⁄₁₆″ turn-under allowance. Fold the seam allowance straight across the point. Bring up your thread through the exact tip of the point, hiding the knot in the fold. Take one stitch in the background.

Hold down the end of the appliqué. Use the shaft of the needle to turn under a portion of the allowance beyond the point, then stitch. Continue stitching to the next point.

Make a stitch at the tip of this point on your appliqué shape. You may take a tiny second stitch here if you like, to secure the piece. Clip off any excess fabric at the point if needed. Push under the allowance using your needle and continue stitching around the piece.

Naturally, some points are sharper than others. Cutting your leaves on the bias is helpful, but if I'm fussy cutting I don't worry about the fabric grain. Enjoy the variations nature brings.

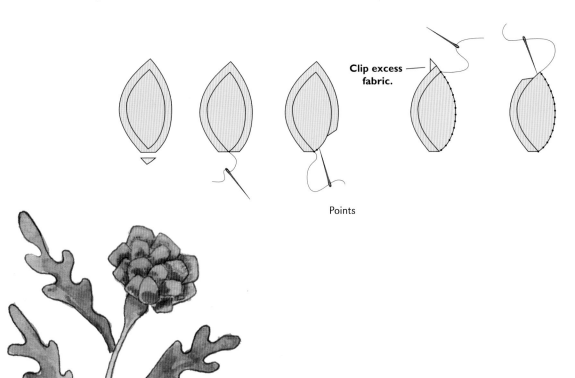

Clip excess fabric.

Points

STEMS

Almost any stem can be appliquéd with bias strips. Of course, stems can also be embroidered if you choose. I note in the individual flower and project instructions which I appliquéd and which I embroidered.

Bias strips are cut on a 45° angle to the straight grain. This makes a piece that stretches and does not easily fray. I often cut only slightly off grain if the stem has little or no curve. When a stem has a tight curve, I cut on the true bias.

Bias Strips

For stitching larger widths, cut the bias strip the width needed plus turn-under on both sides. There is no need to mark the lines on the bias piece; the stem outline on the background is sufficient. Finger-press the allowance under along one side of the bias strip. Stitch the strip in place, following the markings on the background. Then go up the other side, turning the allowance under as you sew. I sew the inside of a curve first when possible.

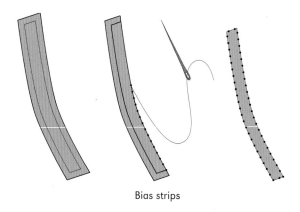

Bias strips

Tiny Bias Strips

For narrow bias strips, cut the strip at least ½″ wide so that the fabric is easy to handle. As with the wider bias, begin by turning under the allowance and stitching down one side. Flip the bias back and trim away any excess allowance, but don't trim too close to the stitching. Flip the bias back in place and trim to twice the width of the stem. Needle-turn the allowance as you stitch down the other side. With some fabric, you can sew a surprisingly thin stem. With other fabric, it can be more challenging. Remember that real stems are not perfectly even at all times.

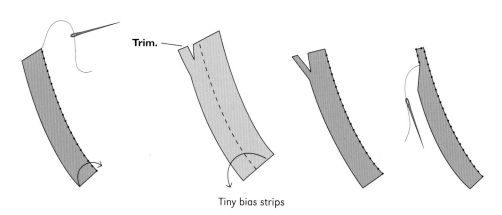

Tiny bias strips

EMBROIDERY

I use four simple stitches for those little details too small for appliqué. I use two strands of floss unless otherwise noted. Use a hoop if you prefer. Add embroidery after the appliqué is complete.

French Knot

The French knot is fabulous for flower centers, stamen ends, and anywhere else dots of color are needed. A seed bead is a great substitute for a French knot.

Bring up the needle from the wrong side of the fabric. Wrap the floss around the needle twice and insert the needle back into the fabric close to the thread's exit. Pull the needle through the fabric, holding the knot until all the floss is pulled through. Pull the knot, but not too tightly. You can increase the size of the knot by using more strands of floss.

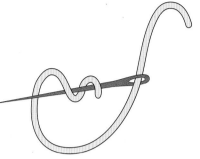

French knot

Stem Stitch

The stem stitch is great stitch for stems (of course), for outlining a piece of appliqué, for flower stamens, or for any line. To make a thicker line, stitch two or more lines next to one another. Want a tiny line? Use a single strand of floss.

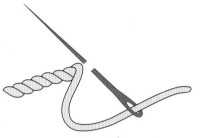

Stem stitch

Satin Stitch

If you need to fill an area with color, satin stitch is the stitch to use.

Straight Stitch

For some flower centers, I use simple long straight stitches. You will find it easier to stitch from the outer end of each stamen to a center point. This makes a nice center with a bit of depth.

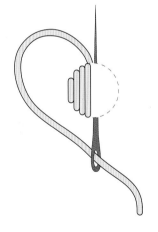

Satin stitch

Borders, Quilting, and Finishing

BORDERS

After the appliqué, embroidery, and embellishment are complete, remove all markings. Press the piece from the back on a padded surface. Use a cutting mat, rotary cutter, and ruler to trim the piece to the required size. Keep it square and remember to include ¼″ seam allowances all around.

To add one or more borders to frame the appliqué, measure your piece for border lengths. Using a ¼″ seam allowance, stitch on the sides first, measure again, and then add the top and bottom.

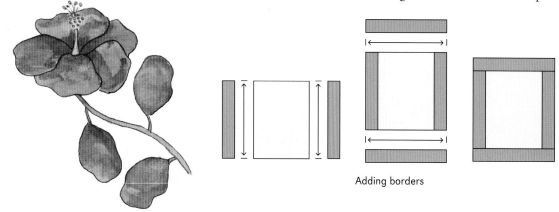

Adding borders

QUILTING

When a light, neutral background is used for an appliquéd quilt, the quilting becomes an integral part of the end result. The shadows and highlights created by the quilting lines make the background rich and alive.

Simple shapes repeated and overlapped create a complex-looking pattern. You can opt for a shape drawn from the appliqué or even one of the patterns on the fabrics. By keeping designs random, you minimize the need for marking. Your quilt lines can also be used to represent rays of sun, raindrops, the movement of water or wind, or extra branches and leaves. It is rather like doodling with a needle and thread.

LAYERING AND BASTING

Cut the backing and batting 1″ larger (or more) than the quilt top on all sides. Lay the backing, right side down, on your basting surface. Place the batting on top of the backing. Then add the quilt top, right side up. Smooth the layers out flat. Use white thread to baste the three layers together in a grid of vertical and horizontal lines, 3″–4″ apart. This grid will keep the layers together, even when you are quilting without a frame or hoop.

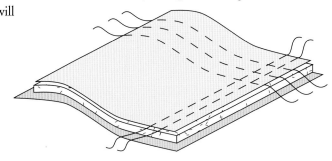

Basting

THE QUILTING STITCH

I use a simple running stitch to quilt, taking several stitches on the needle at a time. I rock both the needle and the fabric.

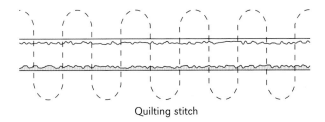

Quilting stitch

Knot approximately 18″ of quilting thread. To begin stitching, pull the knot through the quilt top into the batting and come up to the top again. Give a little tug to bury the knot in the batting. To end, knot the thread close to the quilt top and pull it into the batting. Let the needle travel its length through the batting and come up to the top again. Carefully snip off the thread. I like to travel the needle at a right angle to the line of quilting.

Be careful not to push and pull the layers as you quilt. Keep the work relaxed and trust the basting to hold. This will help you keep a flat quilt with straight edges.

 Tip   I baste on my cutting mat to protect my table from the needle. Cardboard is also a good surface.

MARKING

None of the designs in my projects were marked prior to basting. To repeat a design shape such as a square, cut a template from paper or a nonwoven fabric. Pin the template in place and quilt around it. Reposition the template and quilt around it again. Overlap the shape throughout the background. My designs often ignore the appliqué—when my quilting meets an appliqué, I go under the appliqué, through the batting, and out the other side onto the top, and continue my quilting. (See *24 Flowers* on page 54.)

For quilting straight lines such as rays of sun, I use masking tape and quilt along its edge. Do not leave the tape on for long periods of time. (See *Rose Basket* on page 50.)

For small shapes, you can mark as you go, if needed. One method is to use a blue water-erasable fabric marker and lightly mark a motif or shape freehand. After quilting, remove these marks with a wet paper towel or cotton swab to avoid soaking the quilt. Another method of marking as you sew is to make a small line by pressing the tip of your needle into the fabric. This creates an indentation that lasts long enough to quilt.

QUILTING DESIGNS

Where to begin quilting? In general, I start in the center and work out, or I work from one side and go across to the other. But do not let this inhibit your designing. Once you gain some experience you can experiment more, as you will have more confidence that the basting will keep the layers smooth. I may choose a single shape overlapping across the entire quilt, or I may create sections and add quilting in each. Sometimes I begin at a motif and radiate the design outward, using echo lines, loops, or other shapes. The possible combinations are endless. Try doodling on paper for ideas and keep a quilting ideas library. Pages 59–61 will give you some ideas as well.

BINDING

After quilting, take out the basting threads and remove any markings. Trim the batting and backing flush with the quilt top, keeping the piece square.

I use straight single-fold, cross-grain binding. Cut the strips 2″ wide selvage to selvage. Stitch the binding to the quilt using a ½″ seam. This will result in a ½″ finished bound edge. As with borders, I stitch the binding on the sides of the quilt first, then on the top and bottom.

Turn the binding to the back of the quilt and fold under the raw edge to meet the quilt edge, and then fold again to meet the stitch line on the back of the quilt. Miter the corners following the illustrations. I pin the entire binding in place before hand stitching it down. Use a blind stitch, being careful not to stitch through to the front. Sign and date your wonderful work.

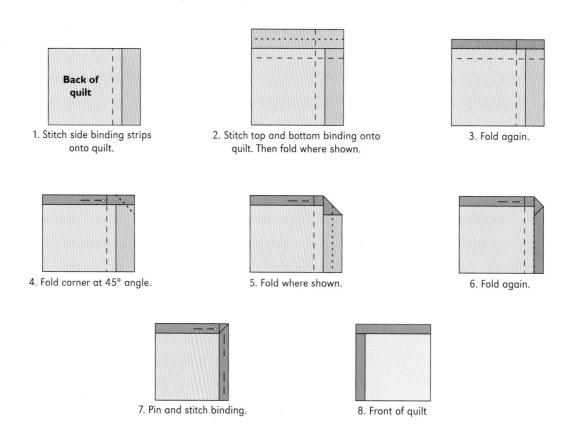

1. Stitch side binding strips onto quilt.

2. Stitch top and bottom binding onto quilt. Then fold where shown.

3. Fold again.

4. Fold corner at 45° angle.

5. Fold where shown.

6. Fold again.

7. Pin and stitch binding.

8. Front of quilt

Binding (fold lines shown in red)

Flowers and Appliqué Patches

DESIGNING A QUILT

Just like planting your own garden, you can take the 24 flowers in this book and combine, repeat, reverse, clip, add, enlarge, and change colors to your heart's content. The same is true of the embellishments; many flower centers work with several different flowers. It's fun to play with the addition of beads, buttons, trims, and paint. There is no right or wrong—if you like it, it's great.

Flowers

When designing a quilt with my flowers, reduce the flower patterns to 50% first. This makes drawing a design quicker. Use a lightbox to trace the flowers onto plain white paper or graph paper. They can overlap or stand alone. When flowers overlap, decide which appears in front by erasing the lines that cross behind. Then color the design using watercolor or colored pencils. There are watercolor drawings scattered throughout the book to inspire you. You can even enlarge them to create your own projects.

Patches

Creating appliquéd patch designs is easiest with graph paper. Use any favorite pieced design with basic shapes. (See *Fence Line Flowers* on page 46 for an example.) Avoid very sharp, long points or too many tiny pieces that can be difficult to appliqué. It's a fun technique but keep it simple.

When you are happy with your half-size drawing, enlarge it to the desired size. A trip to your local copy shop makes quick work of this step.

My stock of half-size designs always exceeds my time to sew, but I always have plenty of patterns at the ready.

Be brave, experiment, and may your garden grow!

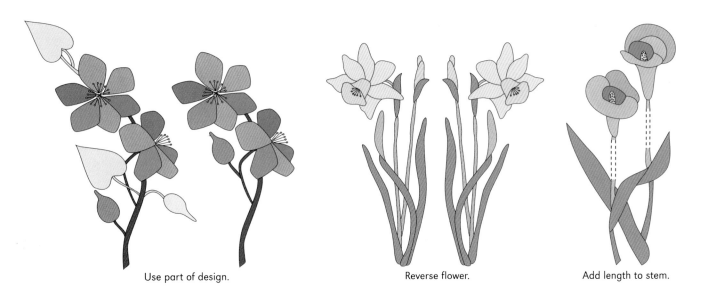

Use part of design.   Reverse flower.   Add length to stem.

Amaryllis

Amazing blooms in red, orange, pink, or white rise from a tall stalk. Lengthen the flower stem to suit your quilt design.

Each piece within an individual flower pattern is numbered according to the order of appliqué. Carefully follow this numbered order. Suggestions for pre-appliqué (see Pre-Appliqué on page 8) and embroidery instructions are also included. When appliquéing stems, follow the guidelines on page 12 for using bias strips. In addition, various embellishment options are offered, which you can mix and match to create your own designs.

Embroidery

Embroider the stamens with a light pink stem stitch. Use a double row of stem stitch for the center stamen. Add straight stitches in yellow to the end of each stamen in a little V shape, and 3 straight stitches perpendicular to the center stamen. To add a bit of dimension, use some dark stitching at the base of the stamens in the color of your flower.

Embellishment

Use beads of various sizes and shapes at the ends of the stamens.

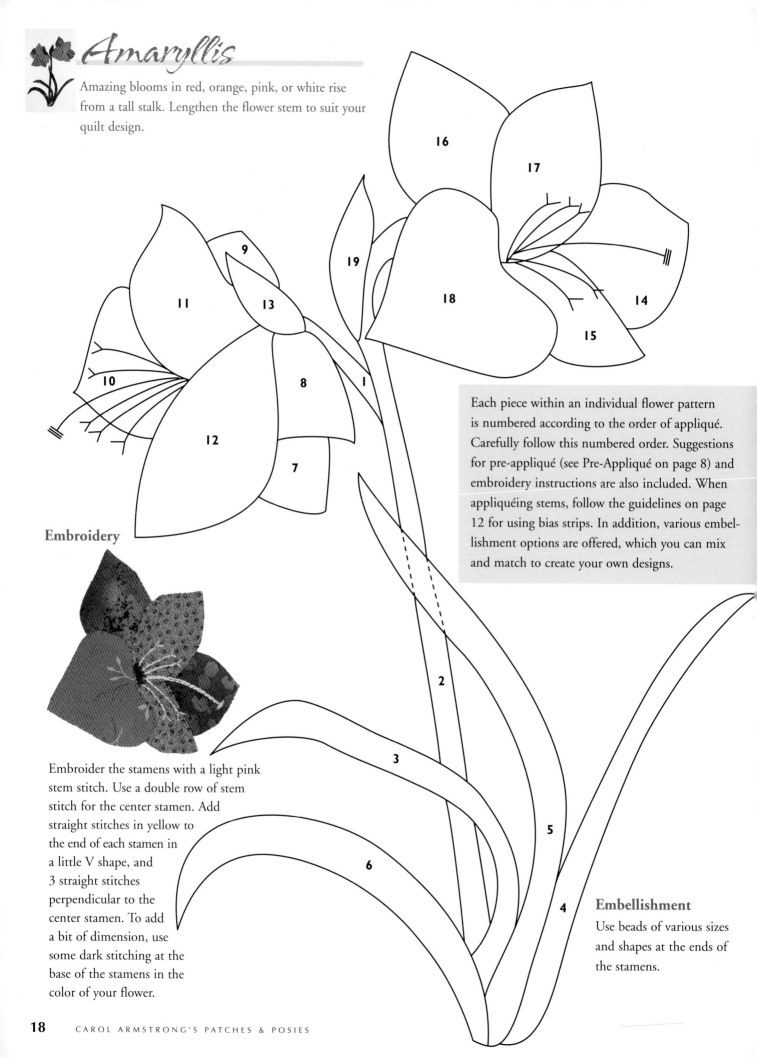

Pre-Appliqué

Pre-appliqué piece #6 onto #5, #11 onto #10, and #16 onto #15, then add #17.

Embroidery

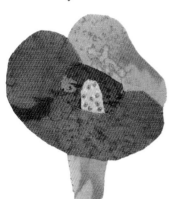

Add several French knots to the flower centers.

Embellishment

Option 1

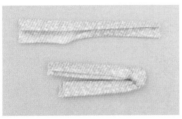

Begin the appliqué and stop before adding the flower centers (pieces #9 and #14). These will be omitted. Cut a 1″× 3″ piece of bias. Fold both long edges toward the center. Press. Fold the strip in half. Press again. Tie a single knot in the center of the strip.

Insert the knotted strip in place of the appliqué flower centers. Trim any excess length to avoid bulk. Cover the raw edges of the knotted strip with the final appliqué piece (#11 or #17). Tack down the top of the knot with a few stitches from the back.

Option 2

Replace the French knots in the flower centers with seed beads for some extra sparkle.

Calla Lily

The calla is a simple but elegant flower. Choose from pinks and reds, whites and creams, yellows and oranges, and lavenders.

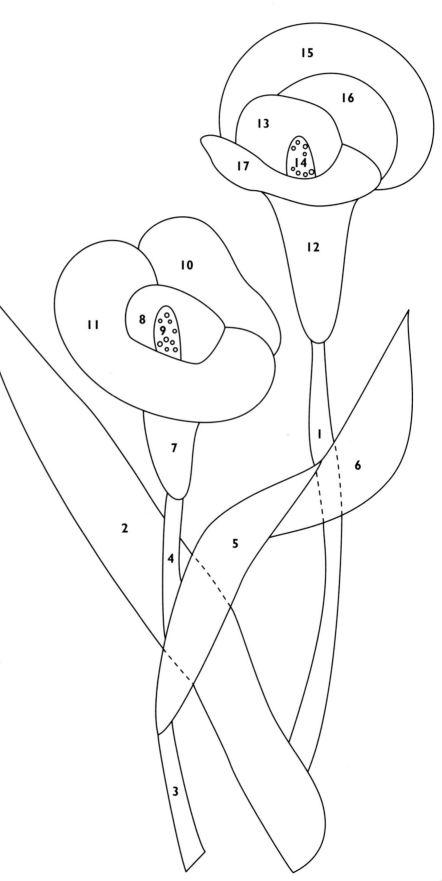

Clematis

There are hundreds of hybrids of this garden vine. Colors include white, pink, red, blue, lavender, or purple with a many-stamened yellow center.

Appliqué

Cut the small leaves (pieces #9 and #10) along the bias for easier handling.

Embroidery

Use long, straight yellow stitches for the centers. End each stitch with a French knot. I like to use 2 different yellows.

Add a black French knot in the open flower center.

Embellishment

Use a tatted circle around a bead for a flower center. Try different thread weights. Thank you to Glynne Ellen, my friend who tats.

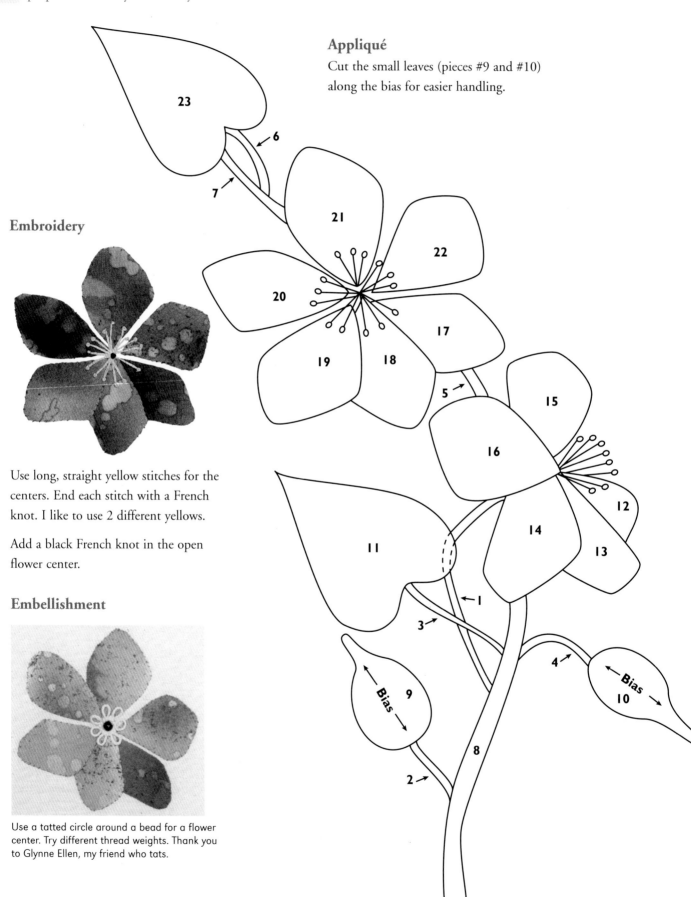

Crocus

The first flower of spring, this little bloom can appear before all the winter's snow has melted. Use yellows, pinks, or purples.

Pre-Appliqué

Pre-appliqué piece #8 onto #7 and #10 onto #9.

Embroidery

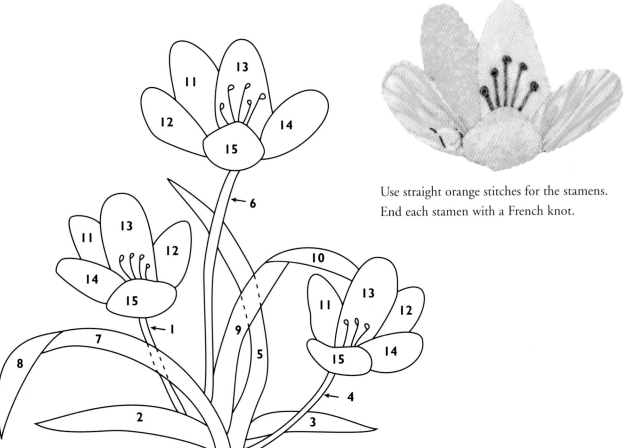

Use straight orange stitches for the stamens. End each stamen with a French knot.

My crocus were fussy cut from this citrus fruit print fabric!

Daffodil

The daffodil is a familiar, graceful spring garden flower. It appears in shades of yellow, orange, white, and even some pinks.

Pre-Appliqué

Pre-appliqué piece #11 onto #10 and #19 onto #18.

Embroidery

Use straight stitches ending with French knots for the center stamens.

Embellishment

Option 1

Do not pre-appliqué piece #19 onto #18. Complete the appliqué through piece #17. Tear a 1″ × 5″ strip of fabric and fringe 1 edge. Trim to ½″ wide, including ⅛″ of fringe.

Place the strip, fringe out, under the needle-turn edge of piece #18 when completing the appliqué. Clip into the unfringed side at the curves, as needed. Add piece #19.

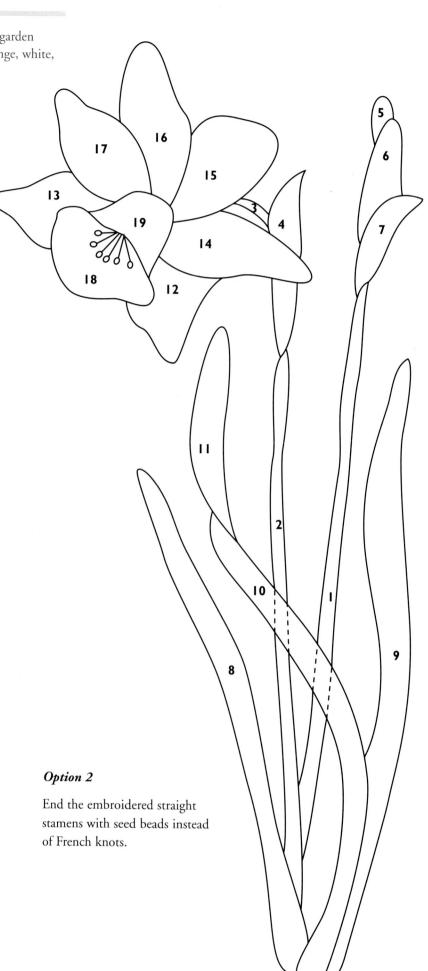

Option 2

End the embroidered straight stamens with seed beads instead of French knots.

Pre-Appliqué

Pre-appliqué piece #4 onto #3.

Embroidery

Use 2 parallel lines of stem stitch in green for the leaf stems. Fill the center area with yellow French knots and 2 black French knots at the very center.

Embellishment

Stitch on a single special button or nestle 2 buttons together in the center. Using 2 strands of floss, add some stitches across the buttons in orange and yellow through the center holes. I also added yellow beads to the flower below.

Dahlia

My garden book says this pixie comes in all colors except true blue. This design does have a lot of little pieces, but slow and steady stitching produces a gorgeous flower. It is well worth the time. I cut out the flower pieces as I sew, using shades of the same color.

Daisy Fleabane

The tiny radiating petals defy appliqué but are perfect when created with fringed cotton fabrics. Whites, pinks, and purples are the palette.

These fringy flowers can be used as centers for other flowers such as zinnia or clematis.

Creating the Flowers

Complete the appliqué through piece #10, remove any marker, and press.

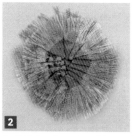

1. Cut a 1¼″ × 5″ strip of fabric. The fabric is easiest to fray when the strips are cut selvage to selvage, across the width of the fabric. Fringe both sides of the strip evenly, leaving a scant ½″ in the center. Fold and press the strip in half lengthwise. Run a gathering thread along the fold.

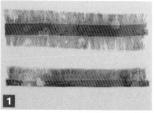

2. Pull the thread and bring the ends of the strip together to form a circle. Secure with several stitches. Trim any wayward fringes, if needed. Press.

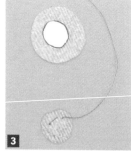

3. Cut a cardstock template for the flower center. Cut a yellow fabric circle larger than the template and stack them together. Run a gathering thread around the fabric circle and draw it up around the template. Do not secure the thread. Press the circle using a bit of spray starch. Loosen the gathering thread and remove the template. Pull the thread a bit and secure.

4. Appliqué the fabric circle onto the center of the fringe circle. Go slowly and carefully to avoid catching the fringe in your stitches. Sew the completed blossom in place from the back of the work with 6 or so stitches going around the thick center area.

Embellishment

Place the fringe circle on the appliquéd stem and stitch a button in the center to hold the circle and the button down on the background.

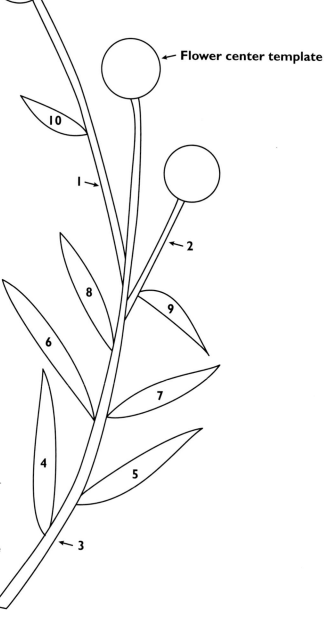

← **Flower center template**

Embroidery

Graceful spikes in pinks, whites, or purples
can grow 3–5 feet tall. Often the inside has
contrasting spots.

Embellishment
Use beads to replace the
French knots.

Embroider the stem at the top
using 2 rows of green stem stitch.
Use yellow straight stitches for the
stamens. End each stamen with a
French knot. Use a fabric marker
to make contrasting color spots in
the lower blossom petals.

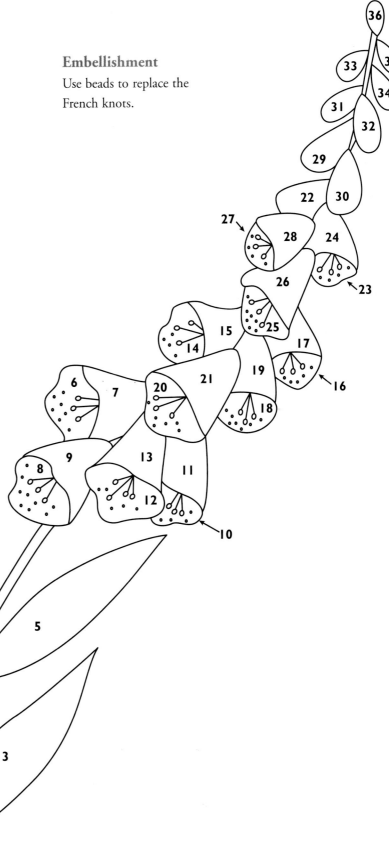

Hibiscus

Also known as Rose of China, this large flower comes in pinks, whites, yellows, oranges, and reds.

(diagram with numbered pieces: 9, 8, 5, 11, 10, 6, 7, 6, 10, 7, 11, 8, 9, 2, 4, 1, 3)

Appliqué

Cut piece #11 along the bias for easier handling.

Embroidery

Use 2 rows of stem stitch for the little leaf stems. Create a cluster of yellow French knots above the center piece. Add pink straight stitches ending with yellow French knots at the top of the flower.

Embellishment

Option 1

Replace the French knots with seed beads.

Option 2

Instead of embroidery, use a pink gel pen to mark the top lines and add a skirt of lines at the base of the center piece. Use dots of yellow 3-D paint to replace the French knots. Allow the paint to dry thoroughly before pressing.

Hosta

The leaves of the Hosta can range from deep green to golden yellow, from solid colors to variegated. Have fun with fabric here. The simple blossoms are white, lavender, or blue.

Embroidery

Use 2 rows of stem stitch for the flower stems.

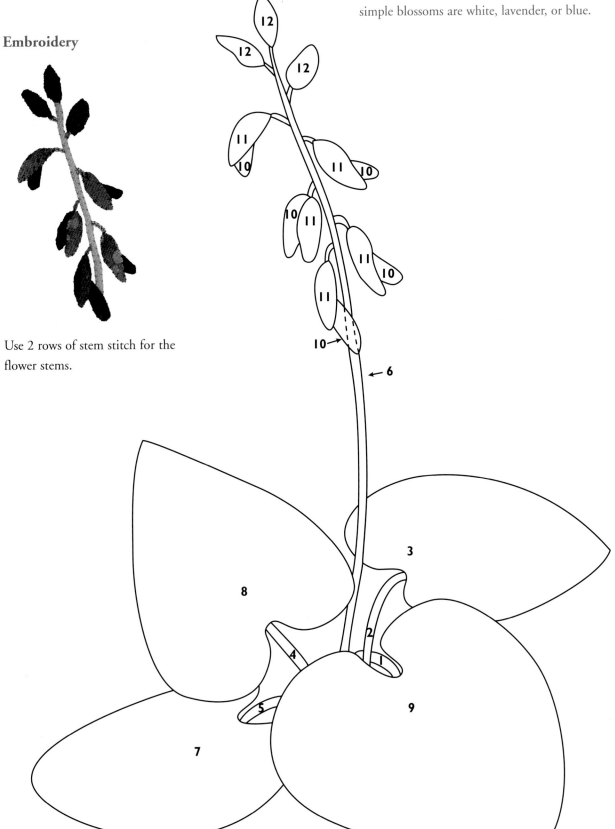

Lupine

Use your favorite colors for these beautiful spires. This hardy plant is often seen growing along country roads.

Embroidery

Add the little stems off the flower stalk using 1 row of green stem stitch.

These creamy white–petaled flowers can be as large as 8″ across. The leaves are equally large and are glossy green. This appliquéd version lacks only the fragrance.

Pre-Appliqué

Pre-appliqué piece #7 onto #6, #15 onto #14, and #17 onto #16.

Embroidery

Appliqué the leaf stems with tiny bias or use 2 parallel lines of green stem stitch to embroider them. Cover the flower center cone with green French knots.

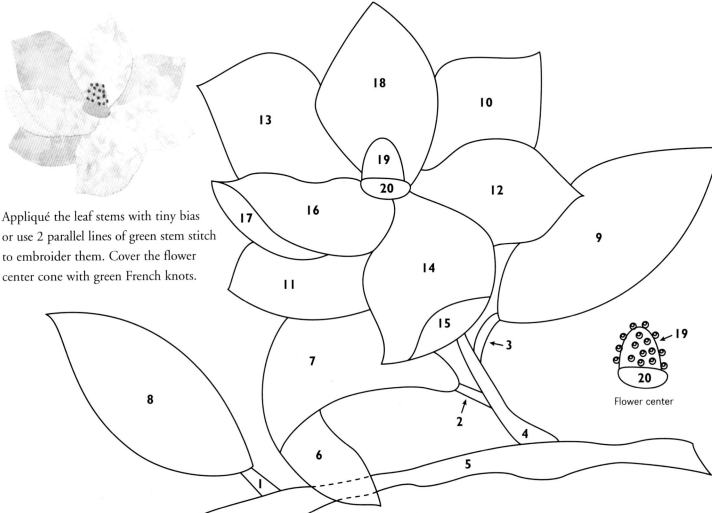

Flower center

Embellishment

Option 1

Complete the appliqué through piece #18. Omit piece #19. Cut a piece of yellow chenille yarn or use silk paint to color white yarn, as I did. Fold the chenille in half.

Place the folded chenille in the place of piece #19, so that #20 will cover the raw ends. Stitch down. Appliqué piece #20, covering the ends of the yarn.

Option 2

Complete the appliqué through piece #18. Omit piece #19. Cut a fabric circle 1½″ in diameter. Run a gathering thread around the circumference. Pull up the center of the circle while pulling the thread. Secure with a few stitches.

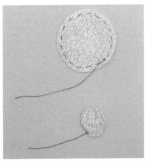

Place this bud-like shape on the appliquéd flower in place of piece #19, so that #20 will cover the raw bottom edges. Stitch in place from the back. Appliqué piece #20, being sure to cover the raw edges.

Marigold

Popular annual flowers, marigolds come in many sizes and shades of orange, yellow, and cream. The leaves are a bit of a challenge with the many inside curves, but relax and accept the varied results.

Appliqué

Note that the stems widen at the top, so allow extra width when cutting the bias strips. Butt the leaves next to the stems.

I remember these delicate trumpet-shaped flowers from when I was a little girl. They grew on a neighbor's trellis. Each blossom lasts only the day.

Embroidery

Use a green stem stitch for the tendrils. Keep your stitches small when going around tight curves. Use white straight stitches in the center of each flower. Finish with 1 black and 1 yellow French knot in the center.

Embellishment

Option 1

Stem stitch around each appliqué piece of the flower. Use a darker or a lighter floss. Add the embroidered flower center.

Option 2

Keep your eyes out for bits of lace at shops and sales. I found a little Irish rose motif on an old collar and cut it out.

Stitch the lace to the flower center. Add beads.

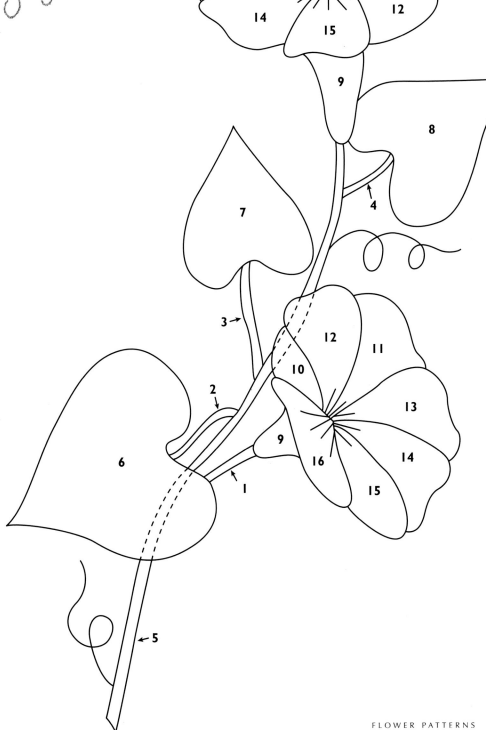

Passion Flower

Embellishment finishes this flower. Use fabric fringe to create the delicate parts of this elegant bloom.

Creating the Flower

1. Complete the appliqué through piece #21. Begin with a 4″ × 2½″ strip of coarse white fabric (I use Osnaburg). Fringe 1 long side until the fringe is about ¾″ long. Cut a 4″ × 1¾″ strip of fusible web and fuse it just above the top of the fringe. Trim the fringed strip to the length of the fringe plus ¼″. Clip along the fused edge, but not all the way through.

2. Cut a 1″-diameter circle from fabric and fuse the fringe around it. The clips along the fused edge allow the strip to curve. Take it bit by bit, using the tip of the iron. You want the top of the fringe to be along the outer edge of the fabric circle.

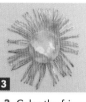

3. Color the fringe with silk paint (or use thinned acrylic paint) and allow it to dry. Heat set the paint. Separate any fringe that has stuck together.

4. Lay the fringed circle in place over the already appliquéd petals. Cut out piece #22 and baste its allowance under. Place this over the fringed circle. Cut a shield from some scrap fabric and pin it over the flower, covering the fringe. This makes sewing the center easier. Appliqué piece #22. Remove the basting. Appliqué or embroider the 4 center yellow pieces (#23). Complete all the embroidery. Remove the shield when done.

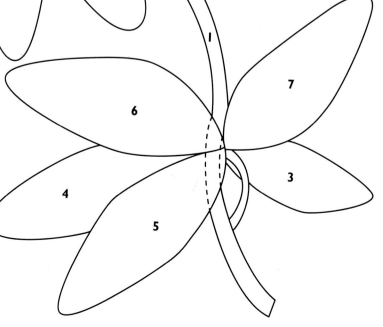

Embroidery

Use pinkish-purple French knots around the center circle and a few straight green stitches in the center yellow pieces. These can be embroidered if tiny appliqué is not your choice. Use 3 rows of green stem stitch for the 2 smaller leaf stems.

Embroidery

Use 2 rows of green stem stitch for the leaf stems. Stitch yellow straight stitches in a fan for the stamens. End each straight stitch with a French knot.

Embellishment

Option 1

Omit the appliqué of the leaves. Finish all the other appliqué, including the stem embroidery. Lengthen the leaf stems about ¼″. Cut out 2 pieces for each leaf with a ¼″ seam allowance. Stitch with right sides together; leave an opening for turning. Trim the seam allowance to ⅛″ and turn the leaf right side out. Press. Stitch, fuse, or glue the opening closed. Use 2 strands of floss to backstitch the leaf to the background through its center. I also appliquéd down the end of the leaf that touched the stem. This method works best with leaves without sharp points. Note: Leaf #6 will now be in front of the flower unless you create it first and appliqué pieces #11, #12, and #16 on top of it.

Peony

These garden blooms come in shades of white, cream, yellow, pink, rose, burgundy, and scarlet. I look forward to these gorgeous flowers in my garden each June.

Option 2

Appliqué the flower through piece #20. Begin with a strip of yellow fabric about 1″ x 1″. Fold it in half, wrong sides together. Press. Open the piece and fringe both sides to ⅛″ from the fold. Refold. Run a small gathering stitch along the folded edge. Pull the thread and gather the fabric into a tuft of fringe. Secure the thread.

Place the folded edge of the tuft of fringe below piece #17 so that #21 will cover it. Stitch in place from the back. Appliqué piece #21, making sure to cover the tuft's folded edge. Continue with the appliqué order.

Option 3

Appliqué the flower through piece #20. Cut a motif from inexpensive lace. Notice the different designs in the examples. I used silk paint to color the lace yellow.

Pin the lace motif with the tail below the bottom of piece #17. Appliqué piece #21, covering the tail of the lace. Continue with the appliqué order. Stitch the lace down in a few spots if it will not stay.

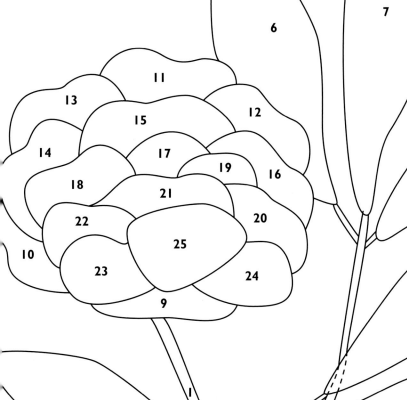

Option 4

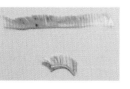

Layer 2 small pieces of decorative yarn. Tack the yarn in place with its base below the bottom of piece #17. Appliqué piece #21, covering the tacking and the non-decorative edge of the yarn.

Flower center

33

Poinsettia

The vibrant Christmas flower we all love can be traditional red or the new colors of pink, gold, or white.

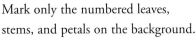

Embroidery

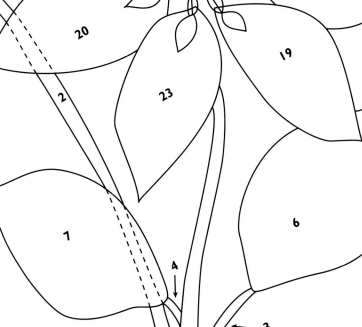

After the appliqué is completed, remove all marks. Press. Return the piece to the lightbox and mark the center design for embroidery. The yellow center pieces can be either appliquéd or embroidered with satin stitch. Use red floss to stem stitch the lines from the ends of the tiny yellow pieces to the center. Use green to satin stitch the little leaflike shapes.

Appliqué

Mark only the numbered leaves, stems, and petals on the background.

Embellishment

Complete the appliqué, omitting the yellow center pieces. Embroider the center red lines. Remove any markings and press. Cut the yellow pieces from faux suede fabric and glue in place with fabric or craft glue. Select some green seed and bugle beads and stitch in the place of the green embroidery.

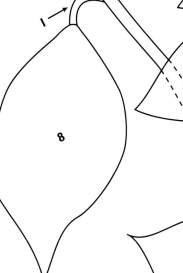

Embroidery

Look, but don't touch. These stunning yellow blossoms grow atop spiny green pads to provide a beautiful splash of color in the spring desert.

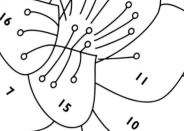

Use groups of 3 straight stitches in beige floss for the spines. Use a white stem stitch for the stamens and tip them with yellow or peach French knots.

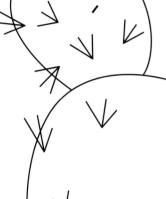

Embellishment

Options 1 and 2

1. To make the pads more dimensional, line the appliqué fabric with 1 or 2 layers of thin batting that is cut to the finished size of the piece. I used a needle-punched polyester batting.

2. To give dimension to the spines, tie them (as if you were tying a quilt) using waxed, heavy thread such as crochet cotton. To hold the knot, wrap the thread twice through the loop before pulling it tight. Trim to length after tying.

Option 3

Stitch the flower through piece #14. Cut about thirteen 1½"-long pieces of perle cotton and knot each of them ⅛" from one end. Line the pieces up on a small strip of fusible web with the knotted ends more or less even. Fuse only the bottom ends together. Place the stamen pieces so that pieces #15 and #16 will cover the fused ends. Tack in place at the base. Approximately 1" of the stamens will stick out from the appliqué. Appliqué pieces #15 and #16.

Redbud

This bright rosy-red flowered tree is at its best in mid to late spring. The flowers open in great abundance before the leaves. Beautiful.

Embroidery

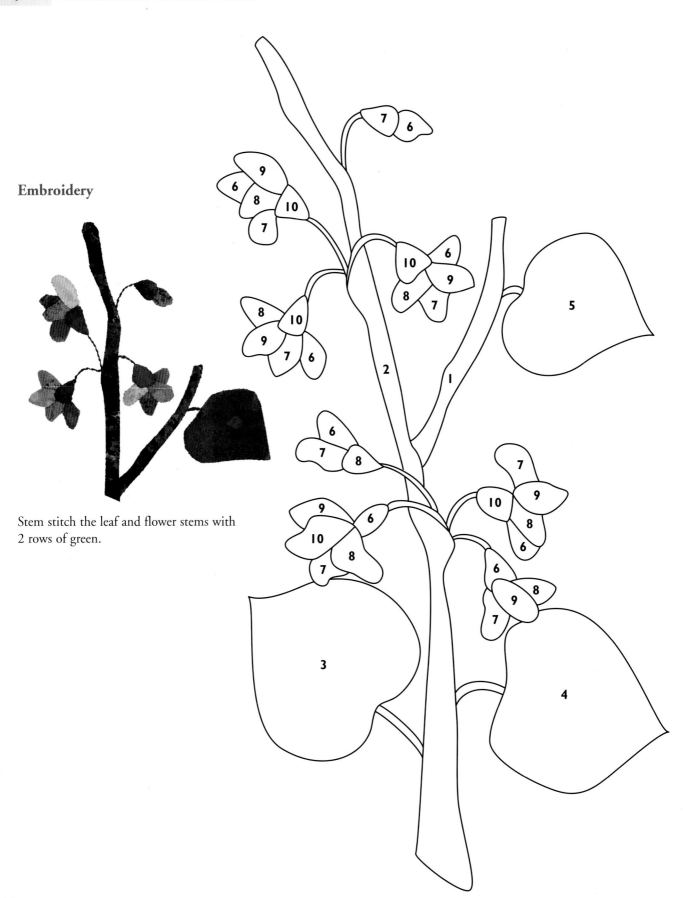

Stem stitch the leaf and flower stems with 2 rows of green.

Rugosa Rose

The Rugosa is a red, pink, or white species of rose. But, of course, you can grow your own cultivar in any color with your artist's license.

Embroidery

Use long, straight yellow stitches for the centers. End each stitch with a French knot. Add some more French knots above the first knots.

Embellishment

Use any center embellishment from a similar flower such as the water lily, peony, or prickly pear. Center the embellishment on piece #25 and cover the bottom ends with piece #29.

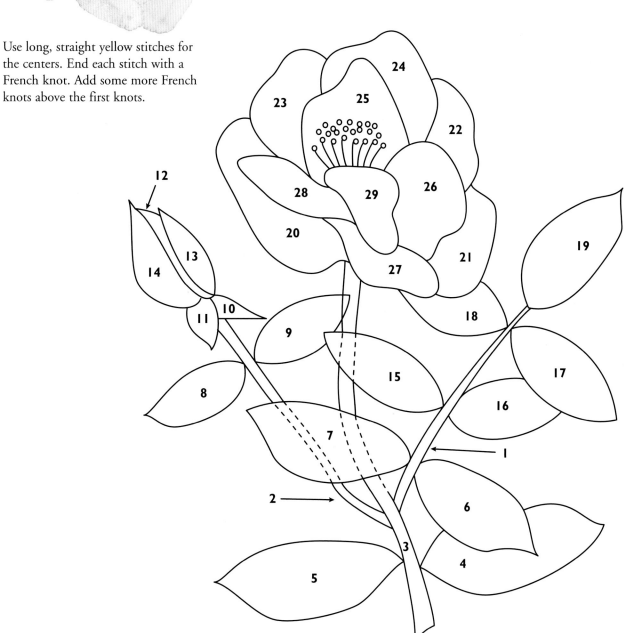

Sedum

Also called stonecrop, these late summer bloomers come in shades of reds, pinks, and rusty oranges. My garden grows one called Autumn Joy. Select prints that look like little clusters of tiny flowers for the flower appliqué.

Appliqué/Embroidery

Appliqué the tiny leaf and flower stems first. (These are not numbered.) Continue by following the numbered appliqué order.

Embellishment

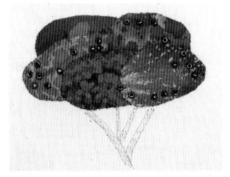

Randomly add some French knots, beads, or both to the flower heads for some texture.

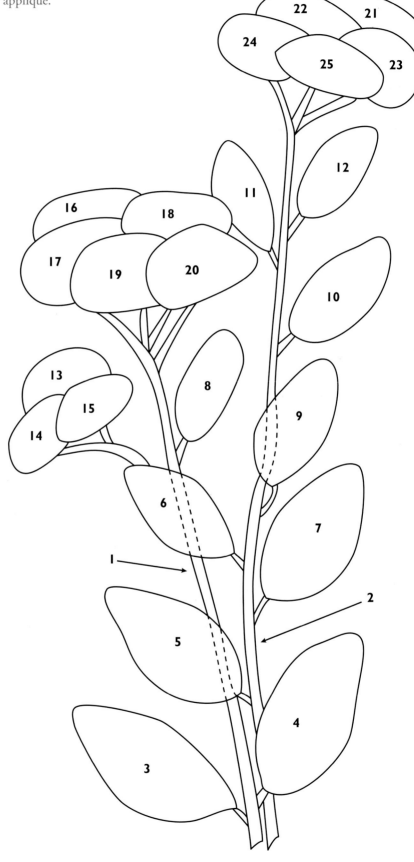

Snapdragon

These tall spikes of color fill many a summer garden. You can choose any of your favorite colors except, as with many flowers, true blue.

Pre-Appliqué

Pre-appliqué piece #3 onto #2 and #6 onto #5.

Embroidery

Use green floss to stitch 2 rows of stem stitch for the little stems. Use yellow straight stitches for each flower's center. Add a dark brown French knot to the very center to add depth.

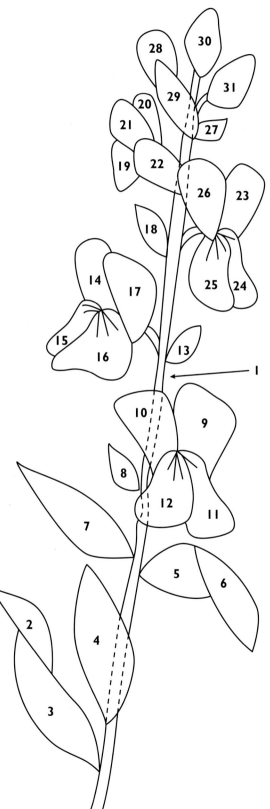

Water Lily

Numerous white petals surround a yellow center to form this gorgeous, fragrant floating flower. Water lilies inhabit quiet water and ponds.

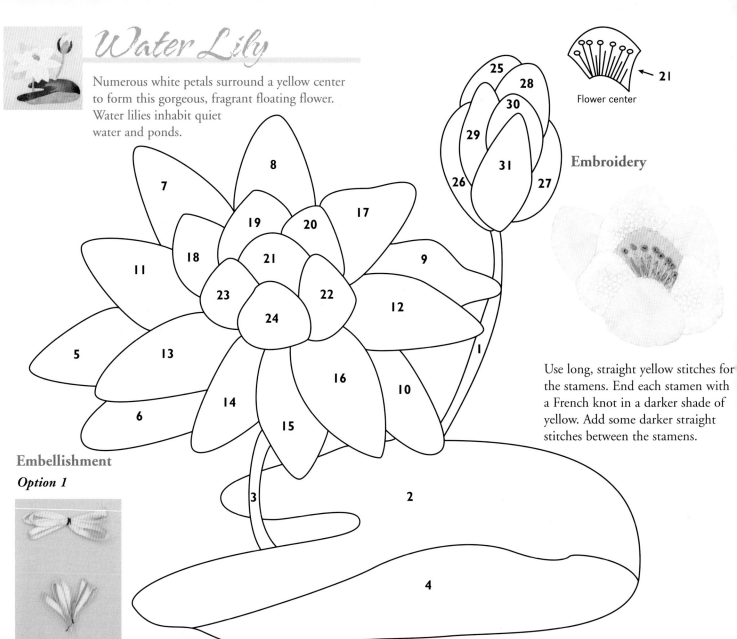

Flower center

← 21

Embroidery

Use long, straight yellow stitches for the stamens. End each stamen with a French knot in a darker shade of yellow. Add some darker straight stitches between the stamens.

Embellishment

Option 1

Appliqué the flower through piece #23. Cut an 8˝ length of ⅛˝-wide ribbon. Make a simple 1½˝-wide bow with 3 loops on each side. Stitch the center together. Trim the tail ends close to the center. Fold the bow in half.

Note: Use thread that matches the fabric; dark thread is used here for demonstration only.

Place the folded edge below the bottom of piece #21 so that #24 will cover the fold. Stitch the fold down. Appliqué piece #24, making sure to cover the folded bottom edge of the ribbon.

Option 2

Appliqué the flower through piece #23. Use approximately 10˝ of 28-gauge craft wire to make a zigzag piece with about 8 bends. Each bend should be about ½˝ long. Pinch the bends together with pliers or your fingers.

Place the bottom loops below the bottom edge of piece #21 so that #24 will cover the loops. Stitch in place, bending the zigzag as you stitch to follow the petal's curve. Appliqué piece #24, making sure to cover the bottom loops of the wire.

Option 3

For the stamens, stitch on bugle beads ending with a seed bead.

Option 4

Use yellow perle cotton to create a fan of straight stitches for the stamens. Add a seed bead to the top of some of them.

Pre-Appliqué

Pre-appliqué piece #2 onto #1, #6 onto #5, and #10 onto #9.

Embroidery

Add a row or more of French knots around the flower center.

Embellishment

Option 1

Use beads to replace the French knots.

Option 2

Add a large button or several buttons layered together in the center.

Option 3

Substitute a small pom-pom for the circle appliqué in the flower center. Stitch it on from the back.

Option 4

Substitute a yo-yo for the circle appliqué in the flower center. Cut a 2″-diameter fabric circle. Run a gathering thread through a tiny hem around the circle edge. Draw it up to form the yo-yo. Add a bead in the middle of the yo-yo. Stitch down at the flower center.

You can pick your color, as the common zinnia comes in all colors, except, of course, blue, as of now. This popular garden plant is one of my favorite summer flowers.

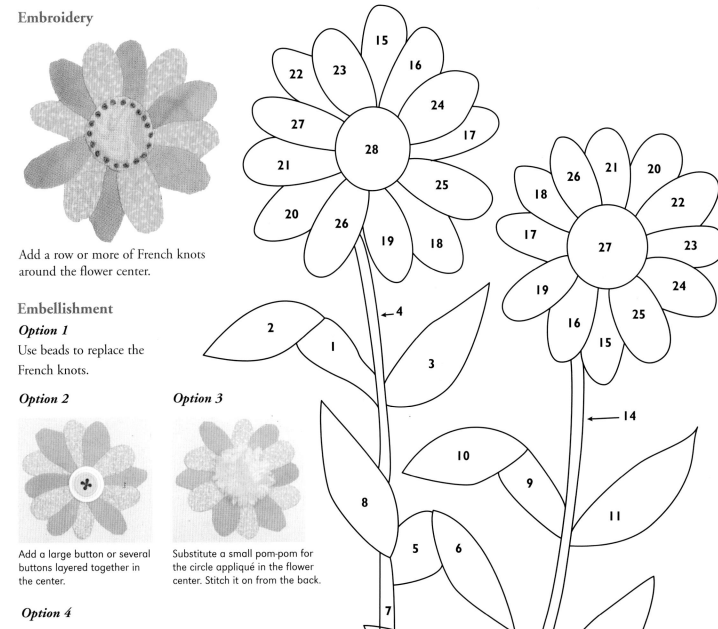

FLOWERS IN THE WINDOW

Finished size 18½″ × 18½″

 Sweet purple crocus with lacy centers appear in this four-pane version of the Attic Window design.

MATERIALS

Muslin background and backing: ¾ yard

Selection of fabrics for appliqué

Inner border: ⅛ yard

Outer border and window frame: ⅓ yard

Binding: ¼ yard

Sewing threads: Colors to match selected fabrics

Quilting thread: Natural color

Lace: Enough to cut out 4 matching motifs

Batting: 22″ × 22″

CUTTING

Muslin background: Cut 1 square 15″ × 15″.

Inner border: Cut 2 strips 1½″ wide selvage to selvage. Measure for exact length before you cut to size.

Outer border: Cut 2 strips 3″ wide selvage to selvage. Measure for exact length before you cut to size.

Binding: Cut 3 strips 2″ wide selvage to selvage. Measure for exact length before you cut to size.

CONSTRUCTION

See pages 7–13 for Lightbox Appliqué Basics.

1. Use a water-erasable fabric marker to mark the block pattern 4 times on the background fabric to form a 4-block design. See page 21 for crocus details. In this project, I've added a lace center instead of embroidered stamens and changed the leaf positions. (The block pattern is on the pullout.)

2. Appliqué the stems, leaves, and flowers first. Note that the raw edges at the bottoms of the stems extend far enough into the appliquéd patch area that they will be covered by the patches. Complete the appliqué order through piece #9.

3. Position the lace motif with the bottom edge extending under piece #10. (See the peony lace embellishment, option 3, on page 33.) Appliqué piece #10.

4. Add the appliquéd patches that create the Attic Window design. (See page 9 for adding appliquéd patches.)

5. Remove all marks. Press.

6. Trim the background to about 12½″ × 12½″, making sure to allow at least ⅜″ to ½″ beyond the appliquéd patches along the edges. When you stitch the borders on using a ¼″ seam, this will allow at least an ⅛″ reveal of the background between the appliquéd patches and the border.

7. Add the borders (see page 14).

8. Baste for quilting (see page 14).

QUILTING

1. Quilt around the appliquéd patches and the inside border.

2. Cut a 5¼″ circle template.

3. Randomly quilt circles all over the background and outer border, allowing them to overlap, creating a crisscross design of circles.

Do not quilt through the flowers, the appliquéd patches, or the inner border.

FINISHING

Trim the quilt layers flush with the edge of the border and bind (see page 16).

DESERT STONES IN BLOOM

Finished size 19½″ × 21″

 Simple pebble shapes in glorious colors complement
the stunning yellow blossom of the prickly pear cactus.

MATERIALS

Muslin background and backing: ⅞ yard

Selection of fabrics for appliqué

Border (non-striped fabric): ¼ yard

OR

Border (striped fabric): ⅝ yard

Binding: ⅓ yard

Sewing threads: Colors to match selected fabrics

Quilting thread: Natural color

⅛″-wide ribbon: 8″

Embroidery floss: Tan

Batting: 21″ × 24″

Optional: Orange gel pen

CUTTING

Muslin background: Cut a rectangle 16″ × 19″.

Border (non-striped fabric): Cut 2 strips 3″ wide selvage to selvage.

OR

Border (striped fabric): Cut 1 strip 3″ wide selvage to selvage for the top and bottom and 2 strips approximately 17″ long parallel to the selvage for the sides. Measure for exact length before you cut to size.

Binding: Cut 4 strips 2″ wide selvage to selvage. Measure for exact length before you cut to size.

CONSTRUCTION

See pages 7–13 for Lightbox Appliqué Basics.

1. Use a water-erasable fabric marker to mark the cactus and pebble design on the background fabric. See page 35 for prickly pear details. In this project, I've used ribbon in the center instead of embroidery. (The pattern is on the pullout.)

2. Appliqué the pebbles in any order in a random color placement.

3. Appliqué the prickly pear through piece #14.

4. Make a ribbon center. (See the water lily ribbon embellishment, option 1, on page 40.)

5. Position this in the flower center and cover the folded ribbon bottom with pieces #15 and #16.

6. Snip the ribbon loops open. Trim to please.

7. If you like, add a little color to the bottom of the ribbons with an orange gel pen.

8. Add the straight-stitch spines in any tan or light color to the cactus pads.

9. Remove all marks. Press.

10. Trim the background to about 14″ × 16½″, making sure to allow at least ⅜″ to ½″ beyond the appliquéd patches along the edges. When you stitch the borders on using a ¼″ seam, this will allow at least an ⅛″ reveal of the background between the appliqué and the border.

11. Add the border with the stripes running vertically (see page 14).

12. Baste for quilting (see page 14).

QUILTING

1. Quilt around the cactus and then add an echo line ¼″ out.

2. Continue around the cactus with thorn shapes and triangles.

3. Quilt wavy, slightly radiating lines of sunshine down from the upper left toward the lower right of the background.

4. Quilt around the pebbles.

5. Stitch 2 parallel lines around the border using 1″ masking tape as a guide.

FINISHING

Trim the quilt layers flush with the edge of the border and bind (see page 16).

FENCE LINE FLOWERS

Finished size 21″ × 19½″

 I chose some bright, cheery colors for this take on the standard Rail Fence design. I also planted some tall flowers with beads added for that bit of sparkle.

MATERIALS

Muslin background and backing: 1⅓ yards

Selection of fabrics for appliqué

Border: ¼ yard

Binding: ⅓ yard

Sewing threads: Colors to match selected fabrics

Quilting thread: Natural color

Embroidery floss: Green, yellow

Seed beads: Orange, yellow

½″ buttons: 2 each of 3 colors, 4 of green

Batting: 24″ × 23″

CUTTING

Muslin background: Cut 1 rectangle 19″ × 18″.

Border: Cut 2 strips 3″ wide selvage to selvage. Measure for exact length before you cut to size.

Binding: Cut 4 strips 2″ wide selvage to selvage. Measure for exact length before you cut to size.

CONSTRUCTION

See pages 7–13 for Lightbox Appliqué Basics.

1. Use a water-erasable fabric marker to mark the Rail Fence design and the flowers on the background fabric. (The pattern is on the pullout.)

2. Appliqué the stems, leaves, and flowers first. Note that the raw edges at the bottoms of the stems extend far enough into the appliquéd patch area that they will be covered by the patches.

- Foxglove: See page 25 for flower details. Replace the French knots with orange seed beads.

- Sedum: See page 38 for flower details. Embroider the little leaf stems. Add yellow seed beads to the blossom.

- Lupine: See page 28 for flower details.

- Snapdragon: See page 39 for flower details. Pre-appliqué piece #4 onto #3. Replace the French knot in the flower center with an orange seed bead.

3. Add the appliquéd patches of the Rail Fence design.

4. Remove all marks. Press.

5. Trim to approximately 17″ × 15½″, making sure to allow at least ⅜″ to ½″ beyond the appliquéd patches along the edges. When you stitch the borders on using a ¼″ seam, this will allow at least an ⅛″ reveal of background between the appliquéd patches and the border.

6. Add the border (see page 14).

7. Baste for quilting (see page 14).

QUILTING

1. Quilt around the appliquéd patches and continue to repeat the Rail Fence design across the background.

2. In the right section beyond the fence design, quilt some veined leaves.

3. Quilt around the flowers.

4. Make a masking-tape template of a leaf and quilt the design randomly around the border, adding a vein to each leaf.

FINISHING

1. Trim the quilt layers flush with the edge of the border and bind (see page 16).

2. Stitch the buttons in the space to the bottom right. I used yellow thread for all and stitched through all 3 layers.

Finished size 11¼″ × 19¾″

 I pulled the flower and the fan colors from my border fabric. This simple little project is quick to stitch. Pick a favorite fabric for your border for inspiration.

MATERIALS

Muslin background and backing: ¾ yard

Selection of fabrics for appliqué

Border: ¼ yard

Binding: ¼ yard

Sewing threads: Colors to match selected fabrics

Quilting thread: Natural color

Seed beads: Orange

Batting: 15″ × 23″

CUTTING

Muslin background: Cut 1 rectangle 10″ × 18″.

Border: Cut 2 strips 3″ wide selvage to selvage. Measure for exact length before you cut to size.

Binding: Cut 2 strips 2″ wide selvage to selvage. Measure for exact length before you cut to size.

CONSTRUCTION

See pages 7–13 for Lightbox Appliqué Basics.

1. Use a water-erasable fabric marker to mark the entire design on the background fabric. See page 19 for calla lily details. I reversed the flower heads and redrew the leaves for this project. (The pattern is on the pullout.)

2. Appliqué the stems, leaves, and flowers first. Note that the raw edges at the bottoms of the stems extend far enough into the appliquéd patch area that they will be covered by the patches. Pre-appliqué #6 onto #5, #11 onto #10, then add #12, and #17 onto #16.

3. Add orange seed beads to the flower centers.

4. Add the appliquéd Grandmother's Fan patch pieces.

5. Remove all marks. Press.

6. Trim to approximately 7¼″ × 15¾″, making sure to allow at least ⅜″ to ½″ beyond the appliquéd patches along the edges. When you stitch the borders on using a ¼″ seam, this will allow at least an ⅛″ reveal of the background between the appliquéd patches and the border.

7. Add the borders (see page 14).

8. Baste for quilting (see page 14).

QUILTING

1. Quilt around the flowers and inside the circle in the center of each flower.

2. Quilt around the fan pieces.

3. Fill the background with overlapping long leaves.

4. Quilt 2 parallel lines around the border, using ¾″ masking tape as a guide.

FINISHING

Trim the quilt layers flush with the edge of the border and bind (see page 16).

ROSE BASKET

Finished size 15″ × 16″

 Roses are a much-loved flower and the basket design is the perfect setting. Use your favorite color of rose to fill your basket.

MATERIALS

Muslin background and backing: ⅔ yard

Selection of fabrics for appliqué

Border: ¼ yard

Binding: ¼ yard

Sewing threads: Colors to match selected fabrics

Quilting thread: Natural color

Fringy specialty yarn: 1 small piece

Batting: 17″ × 18″

Optional: Orange gel pen

CUTTING

Muslin background: Cut 1 rectangle 13″ × 14″.

Border: Cut 2 strips 3″ wide selvage to selvage. Measure for exact length before you cut to size.

Binding: Cut 2 strips 2″ wide selvage to selvage. Measure for exact length before you cut to size.

CONSTRUCTION

See pages 7–13 for Lightbox Appliqué Basics.

1. Use a water-erasable fabric marker to mark the entire design on the background fabric. See page 37 for rose details. I rearranged the rose leaves and stems and omitted the bottom calyx on the bud. Decorative yarn creates the stamens in the center. (The pattern is on the pullout.)

2. Appliqué the stems, leaves, and flowers first. Note that the raw edges at the bottoms of the stems extend far enough into the appliquéd patch area that they will be covered by the patches.

3. Complete the appliqué of each flower through piece #22. Use a fringy yarn for the center stamens. Follow the directions for the peony decorative yarn embellishment, option 4, on page 33. Cover the yarn ends with piece #23.

4. If you like, add a little color to the base of the fringe with an orange gel pen.

5. Add the appliquéd patches of the Flower Basket design.

6. Remove all marks. Press.

7. Trim the background to approximately 11″ × 12″. Start trimming at the bottom, parallel with the basket base, and make sure there is approximately 1¼″ of background beneath the basket. Also make sure the basket is centered, with about 1½″ of background on each side.

8. Add the border (see page 14).

9. Baste for quilting (see page 14).

QUILTING

1. Quilt around the roses and the pieces of the basket.

2. Use the point where the 3 full squares in the basket meet as a center point, and quilt radiating lines outward from there through the border. Use masking tape as a guide.

FINISHING

Trim the quilt layers flush with the edge of the border and bind (see page 16).

AMARYLLIS IN RED

Finished size 16½″ × 19½″

 Red is always a happy color to stitch! Use rich reds when creating this wonderful flower and the companion triangles.

MATERIALS

Muslin background and backing: ¾ yard

Selection of fabrics for appliqué

Border: ¼ yard

Binding: ¼ yard

Sewing threads: Colors to match selected fabrics

Quilting thread: Natural color

6mm pearl beads: 9

Bugle beads: 2 gold

Embroidery floss: Yellow

Batting: 20″ × 23″

CUTTING

Muslin background: Cut 1 rectangle 15″ × 18″.

Borders: Cut 2 strips 3″ wide selvage to selvage. Measure for exact length before you cut to size.

Binding: Cut 2 strips 2″ wide selvage to selvage. Measure for exact length before you cut to size.

CONSTRUCTION

See pages 7–13 for Lightbox Appliqué Basics.

1. Use a water-erasable fabric marker to mark only the stem, leaves, and flower on the background fabric. The triangle patches will be marked later. See page 18 for amaryllis details. For this project, the amaryllis stem is lengthened by approximately 4″. (The pattern is on the pullout.)

2. Appliqué the stems, leaves, and flowers.

3. Replace the embroidered stamen ends with a bugle bead at the end of each large stamen and a pearl bead at the end of each of the others.

4. Remove all marks. Press.

5. Trim the background to 12½″ × 15½″, centering the flower.

6. Add the borders (see page 14). Mark and appliqué the triangle patches. (See page 9 for adding appliquéd patches after borders.)

7. Remove all marks. Press.

8. Baste for quilting (see page 14).

QUILTING

1. Quilt the large feather design first. Begin with the main feather stem and add the feathers from the top down on both sides.

2. Quilt around the outside of the background and around the triangles. Echo quilt ¼″ out from the triangles.

3. Fill in the remaining spaces with large petal shapes coming out from the feather. I also used this design in the border. The petals are all slightly different, as I drew them as I quilted.

FINISHING

Trim the quilt layers flush with the edge of the border and bind (see page 16).

24 FLOWERS

Approximate finished size 40″ × 49″

 The glorious color splash of all 24 flowers forms this design. Accent the bright blooms with alternating squares and half-square triangles in colors pulled from the leaves and blossoms.

MATERIALS

Muslin background and backing: 3⅛ yards

Selection of fabrics for appliqué

Binding: 1¾ yards

Sewing threads: Colors to match selected fabrics

Quilting thread: Natural color

Batting: 42″ × 52″

CUTTING

Muslin background: Cut 1 rectangle the width of the fabric × 52″. More is better here; if things shift you will be able to square the piece.

Square patches: Cut approximately 18 squares, 2¼″ × 2¼″.*

Triangle patches: Cut approximately 17 squares, 2½″ × 2½″. Cut these squares in half diagonally.*

Binding: Cut 4 strips 2″ wide × the length of the fabric. Measure for exact length before you cut to size.

The number of patches will vary depending on your flower placement.

CONSTRUCTION

See pages 7–13 for Lightbox Appliqué Basics.

1. Mark only the stems, leaves, and flowers to begin. It is easiest to make full-size copies of the flower patterns and lay them out on the background fabric in a pleasing design. Use the photo as a guide. Be sure to allow extra fabric around the flowers for the patches and the binding. Allow at least 5½″ extra at the top and 3″ along each of the other 3 edges. Mark the flower patterns on the background fabric using a water-erasable fabric marker. For patterns and flower details, see pages 18–41.

2. Appliqué and embellish each flower as you like, referring to the individual flower instructions.

3. Remove all marks. Press.

4. Trim, leaving approximately 4½″ above the flowers at the top of the piece and 2″ beyond the flowers on the other 3 sides. Be sure the corners are square.

5. To align the patches around the outside edges, measure and mark a line 4″ down from the top and 4″ in from the right side. Then measure again and mark a line 2″ down from the top and 2″ in from the right side. Mark these strips in 2″ increments. I had 19 squares across the top and 16 squares down. A large, wide ruler will help in this marking. I also marked every other square in half diagonally.

6. Appliqué the patches, aligning them inside the marked lines. (See Appliqué Patches on page 9.) I used various colors in the half-square triangles and greens in the squares.

7. Remove all marks. Press.

8. Baste for quilting (see page 14).

QUILTING

1. Use a water-erasable fabric marker to mark a stop-quilting line around the outside of the quilt. Make sure the line is at least 1″ outside any appliqué.

2. Cut a 2″ × 2″ square from paper. Use this as a quilting template. Keep moving the square and quilting around it. Overlap previous squares but don't cross over into previous squares with quilting. Fill the entire background.

3. Go back and quilt a diagonal line in each quilted square or partial square.

4. Quilt around the appliquéd patches.

FINISHING

1. Trim the quilt just outside your stop-quilting line. The size of this quilt will vary according to your appliqué placement. Mine was 40″ × 49″. When you stitch the binding on using a ½″ seam, allow at least a ⅛″ reveal of the background between the appliquéd patches and the binding.

2. Bind (see page 16).

CRAZY ABOUT DAFFODILS

Finished size 16½″ × 16½″

 Add some daffodils, some crazy patches, and a few
embellishments to make a fun project. Any flower
could be used for this appliquéd version of a crazy quilt.

MATERIALS

Muslin for background and backing: ⅔ yard

Selection of fabrics for appliqué

Border: ¼ yard

Binding: ¼ yard

Sewing threads: Colors to match selected fabrics

Quilting thread: Black

A few buttons and seed beads

Batting: 20″ × 20″

CUTTING

Muslin background: Cut 1 square 15″ × 15″.

Border: Cut 2 strips 3″ wide selvage to selvage. Measure for exact length before you cut to size.

Binding: Cut 2 strips 2″ wide selvage to selvage. Measure for exact length before you cut to size.

CONSTRUCTION

See pages 7–13 for Lightbox Appliqué Basics.

1. Use a water-erasable fabric marker to mark the entire block design on the background fabric. See page 22 for daffodil details. I've reversed 2 flower heads and rearranged the leaves for this project. (The pattern is on the pullout.)

2. Appliqué the stems, leaves, and flowers first. Note that the raw edges of the bottoms of the stems and leaves extend far enough into the appliquéd patch area that they will be covered by the patches. I added green seed beads on the stamen ends to replace the French knots.

3. Add the appliquéd patches (see page 9).

4. Remove all marks. Press.

5. Trim the background to approximately 12½″ × 12½″, making sure to allow at least ⅜″ to ½″ beyond the appliquéd patches. When you stitch on the borders using a ¼″ seam, this will allow at least an ⅛″ reveal of the background between the appliquéd patches and the border.

6. Add the borders (see page 14).

7. Baste for quilting (see page 14).

QUILTING

1. Quilt around the appliquéd patches and the flowers.

2. Add a line of quilting around the border 1″ from the inside, using masking tape as a guide.

FINISHING

1. Trim the quilt layers flush with the edge of the border and bind (see page 16).

2. Add some buttons, stitching through all 3 layers.

ANOTHER IDEA

Here's an idea for a quilt combining an appliquéd patch pattern
with each flower. I am sure you will think of more combinations.

In her latest book, Carol Armstrong goes back to the garden to give us more charming flowers and new embellishment ideas. Carol and her cabinetmaker husband enjoy a creative homestead life in Michigan's Upper Peninsula, where the long, snowy winters give her lots of time for creating and quilting.

Since teaching herself to quilt in 1980, Carol has developed her own artistic style, but she credits nature for being an unending source of ideas. But developing these ideas is not all that occupies her time. When she needs a break from her creative pursuits, there is water to pump and bring into the house, wood to load into the wood box, bird feeders to fill, or the large organic vegetable garden to tend.

Other Books by Carol Armstrong

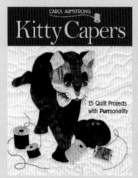

INDEX

Great Titles
from C&T PUBLISHING

fast fun & easy
FABRIC FLOWERS
Karen Flamme
Beautiful Blooms in an Afternoon

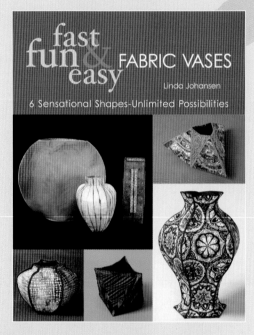

fast fun & easy
FABRIC VASES
Linda Johansen
6 Sensational Shapes-Unlimited Possibilities

All-in-One **Beading** Buddy

The **ultimate** beading reference tool!

Easy to use
Bead Guide
Stitch Index

• 78 Beading Stitches
• Step-by-Step Instructions
• Helpful Tips and How-To's
• Bonus-Value Finder

IDEAL FOR:
Beading
Quilting
Scrapbooking
Embroidery
Wearables
Crafts
Home Décor

Mary Stori

dimensional DELIGHTS
20 Folding Fabric Screens to Personalize, Embellish + Display

Liz Aneloski

Available at your local retailer or
www.ctpub.com or 800.284.1114